BILLIE EILISH

Making a Difference with Her Music

By Katie Kawa

People Who Make a Difference

KidHaven PUBLISHING

Published in 2026 by
KidHaven Publishing, an Imprint of Greenhaven Publishing, LLC
2544 Clinton St.
Buffalo, NY 14224

Designer: Deanna Lepovich
Editor: Katie Kawa

Photo credits: Cover Kathy Hutchins/Shutterstock.com; pp. 5, 13, 15 Sipa USA/Alamy Stock Photo; p. 7 Everett Collection Inc/Alamy Stock Photo; p. 9 MediaPunch Inc/Alamy Stock Photo; p. 11 UPI/Alamy Stock Photo; p. 17 JEP Live Music/Alamy Stock Photo; p. 18 ZUMA Press, Inc./Alamy Stock Photo; p. 20 PA Images/Alamy Stock Photo; p. 21 T.Sumaetho/Shutterstock.com.

Library of Congress Cataloging-in-Publication Data

Names: Kawa, Katie, author.
Title: Billie Eilish : making a difference with her music / Katie Kawa.
Description: [First.] | Buffalo, New York : KidHaven Publishing, 2026. | Series: People who make a difference | Includes index.
Identifiers: LCCN 2025010834 | ISBN 9781534549623 (library binding) | ISBN 9781534549616 (paperback) | ISBN 9781534549630 (ebook)
Subjects: LCSH: Eilish, Billie, 2001–Juvenile literature. | Singers–United States–Biography–Juvenile literature. | LCGFT: Biographies.
Classification: LCC ML3930.E35 K38 2026 | DDC 782.42164092 [B]–dc23/eng/20250314
LC record available at https://lccn.loc.gov/2025010834

Printed in the United States of America

CPSIA compliance information: Batch #CSKH26: For further information contact Greenhaven Publishing LLC at 1-844-317-7404.

CONTENTS

USING HER VOICE

Music has the power to make a difference. Songs can move people, **inspire** people, and make people feel less alone. Billie Eilish knows this. As a teenager, she first became famous for making music that resonated, or connected, with other teenagers who felt like they didn't fit in.

Billie has also found ways to use her voice beyond her songs. She often speaks out about issues many young people care about, including women's rights, bullying, **mental** health, and the **environment**. Through her music and her **activism**, Billie Eilish has become a powerful voice for young people and the things that matter to them.

In Her Words

"The truth is, we can all make change. And I have this platform [ability to talk publicly] and I'm going to use it."

— Interview with *Vogue* magazine from October 2024

Many of Billie Eilish's songs deal with hard things she's gone through as a young person. These songs have helped her fans deal with hard times they're facing in their own lives.

A TALENTED FAMILY

Billie Eilish Pirate Baird O'Connell was **encouraged** to follow her passions, or interests, from a young age. She was born on December 18, 2001, in Los Angeles, California. Her parents, Maggie Baird and Patrick O'Connell, were actors who also loved music. They wanted their children, Billie and her older brother Finneas, to find their own interests, so they chose to homeschool the siblings.

Billie loved to dance, but she gave up her dreams of a future as a dancer after an **injury**. However, she also had an interest in music and began writing her own songs.

In Her Words

"My whole existence [life] is based around family, but especially my mom ... It's thanks to her that I know anything."

— Interview with *Vogue* magazine from January 2023

Billie is shown here with her mom at an event in 2022. They both care deeply about the environment and work together to raise awareness about environmental issues, such as **climate change**.

EARLY SUCCESS

Finneas also had an interest in music, and when Billie was 13, they began recording songs together. In 2015, their song "Ocean Eyes" was released, or put out, online. Billie's **unique** voice made it stand out, and it quickly became popular.

People in the music business began to pay attention to Billie as an artist. In 2016, Billie signed with a record company, and the next year, she released an EP titled *Don't Smile at Me*. This EP, which is like an album with fewer songs, was a hit, and Billie was on her way to becoming the next big thing in the music business.

In Her Words

"I was 13 when I put stuff out for the first time. I look back at who I was, when fewer eyes were on me ... I strive [try] to be that kid again."

— Interview with *Vogue* magazine from January 2023

Billie and Finneas, who's shown here with her, have been making music together for more than 10 years. They still write songs together!

THE FIRST ALBUM

Billie continued to release new songs and gain new fans. Her fame reached new heights in 2019, when her first album was released. *When We All Fall Asleep, Where Do We Go?* featured hit songs such as "Bad Guy," and reached the top of the Billboard 200 chart, which ranks the most popular albums in the United States.

In 2020, Billie became the youngest person to win the four main Grammy Awards—the biggest prizes in the music business. These are Best New Artist, Record of the Year, Song of the Year, and Album of the Year.

In Her Words

"The truth is that ... *the love of my life* is singing."

— Interview with *Vogue* magazine from October 2024

Billie is shown here with Finneas at the Grammy Awards in 2020. She shared many of the awards she won that night with him. *When We All Fall Asleep, Where Do We Go?* was also named Best Pop Vocal Album at the 2020 Grammy Awards, which meant Billie won five Grammys that night.

AN IMPORTANT MESSAGE

The hits kept coming for Billie. In 2021, she won another Grammy for Record of the Year for her song "Everything I Wanted." Later that year, she released her second album, *Happier Than Ever*, which also became a huge success.

One of the songs on *Happier Than Ever* got special attention for its message about body shaming, which is the practice of treating someone unkindly or judging them unfairly because of what their body looks like. "Not My Responsibility" is a song about how hurtful body shaming can be, and Billie also made a video with this song to illustrate this issue for her fans.

Billie has talked openly about being judged for how she looks and the ways she dresses. "Not My Responsibility" is a song about the pain those kinds of judgments can cause. This song has helped many people, especially young women, feel seen as they struggle with body shaming in their own lives.

In Her Words

"Though you've never seen
my body, you still judge it
And judge me for it.
Why?"

— "Not My Responsibility"

A VOICE FOR WOMEN

"Not My Responsibility" is just one example of the ways Billie has used her voice to connect with women over issues that matter to them. In addition, her song "Your Power" is about the ways powerful men can hurt women, calling attention to an issue many women around the world have dealt with.

Billie has also spoken openly about her own struggles with body image. This has helped many women who also have a hard time with the thoughts and feelings they have about their body. In addition, she's used her platform to fight for women's rights in areas such as health care.

In Her Words

"My body is actually me. And it's not out to get me."

— Interview with *Vogue* magazine from January 2023

Billie's unique style has inspired many young women to find their own way of expressing themselves through their clothing.

AN OUTSPOKEN ARTIST

Billie is known for saying what she really thinks and feels—both in her music and in her life. This is why so many young people have connected with her songs. They **appreciate** the honest way she writes about hard things, such as struggles with her mental health. Billie has also been open about living with a condition known as **Tourette syndrome**, and her openness has meant a lot to other people living with this condition.

Billie is also outspoken about politics, or her ideas about the government and its leaders. She has encouraged her fans to make their voices heard by voting.

In Her Words

"If I was happy in my life, it was because people loved me on the internet. And if I was upset in my life, it was usually because people didn't ... I've learned to not base my life around that."

— Interview with *Vogue* magazine from October 2024

Billie has been open about ways fame has hurt her mental health. She has worked hard to separate how strangers online see her from how she sees herself, and she encourages her fans to do the same.

AN ENVIRONMENTAL ACTIVIST

Animal rights are also important to Billie, and she cares deeply about protecting the natural world—keeping it safe. Like many young people today, Billie is worried about the dangers of climate change and wants to do what she can to keep it from getting worse.

Billie has called on world leaders to take action to fight climate change, and she has also called on the music business to do the same. She's even hosted yearly "Overheated" events with her mom. At these events, people can learn more about **sustainability** and actions they can take to fight climate change.

The Life of Billie Eilish

2001
Billie Eilish Pirate Baird O'Connell is born in Los Angeles on December 18.

2015
Billie has her first hit song with "Ocean Eyes."

2017
Billie releases her first EP, *Don't Smile at Me*.

2019
Billie's first album, *When We All Fall Asleep, Where Do We Go?*, is released.

2020
Billie wins five Grammy Awards.

2021
Billie wins another Record of the Year Grammy Award and releases her second album, *Happier Than Ever*.

2022
Billie wins her first Academy Award for the song "No Time to Die," and music she wrote appears in the Pixar movie *Turning Red*.

2024
Billie wins another Academy Award and two Grammy Awards for the song "What Was I Made For?" and releases her third album, *Hit Me Hard and Soft*.

In Her Words

"If you're going to think I'm a role model [someone to look up to], think I'm a role model in terms of trying to save the environment."

— Interview with *Rolling Stone* magazine from April 2024

Only 10 years after releasing her first song, Billie Eilish has become one of the most successful and famous musicians in the world.

MORE MUSIC

Billie has found new audiences for her music through the movies. In 2022, she won an Academy Award—the biggest prize in the movie business—for the song "No Time to Die," which she wrote for the movie *No Time to Die*. That same year, songs she wrote with Finneas appeared in the Pixar movie *Turning Red*. Billie won another Academy Award, along with two Grammys, for "What Was I Made For?" from *Barbie*.

In 2024, Billie released her third album, *Hit Me Hard and Soft*. Her music continues to inspire and move her fans, making a big difference in the lives of many people.

In Her Words

"I feel like I'm becoming a person I really love and doing things I feel really proud of. In many ways in my life, I feel like I'm just now waking up."

— Interview with *Variety* magazine from November 2023

Be Like Billie Eilish!

Learn more about climate change, and talk to people in your life about ways you can help the environment.

Practice sustainability in ways that can include recycling and giving away old clothes instead of throwing them out.

Write to government leaders about the importance of fighting climate change.

Raise money for groups that support women's rights, work to protect the environment, or fight bullying.

If you or someone you know is struggling with mental health, body image, or body shaming, tell a trusted adult.

Leave only kind messages and comments online, and never comment on someone's body.

If someone you know is going through a hard time, write them a letter, a poem, or a song to help them feel less alone.

Write about issues that matter to you. You could even try writing a song about them!

Billie Eilish uses her voice to make a difference. These are just some ways you can make a difference too!

GLOSSARY

activism: Acting strongly in support of or against an issue.

appreciate: To value and be thankful for something.

climate change: Change in Earth's weather caused by human activity.

encourage: To make someone more likely to do something.

environment: The natural world around us.

injury: Harm done to the body.

inspire: To move someone to do something great.

mental: Relating to the mind.

sustainability: The practice of living in a way that is not wasteful.

Tourette syndrome: A disorder that causes people to move or make sounds in a way that cannot be easily controlled.

unique: Special or different from anything else.

FOR MORE INFORMATION

WEBSITES

GRAMMY.com: Billie Eilish

www.grammy.com/artists/billie-eilish/251741

The official website of the Grammy Awards provides facts about all the awards Billie has won and news stories about her music.

IMDb: Billie Eilish

www.imdb.com/name/nm8483808/

The Internet Movie Database offers visitors a list of all the movies and TV shows Billie's songs have appeared in, as well as facts about her life and news stories about her.

BOOKS

Bell, Samantha. *Billie Eilish*. St. Catharines, Ontario: Crabtree Publishing, 2025.

Gardiner, Nora. *Billie Eilish*. Buffalo, NY: Enslow Publishing, 2022.

Nguyen, Suzane. *Billie Eilish*. Minneapolis, MN: Bellwether Media, 2025.

Publisher's note to educators and parents: Our editors have carefully reviewed these websites to ensure that they are suitable for students. Many websites change frequently, however, and we cannot guarantee that a site's future contents will continue to meet our high standards of quality and educational value. Be advised that students should be closely supervised whenever they access the internet.

INDEX